I0503238

LINUX Operating System success in a day

By Sam Key

Beginners guide to fast, easy and efficient learning of LINUX Operating Systems

2nd Edition

Copyright 2015 by Sam Key - All rights reserved.

In no way is it legal to reproduce, duplicate, or transmit any part of this document in either electronic means or in printed format. Recording of this publication is strictly prohibited and any storage of this document is not allowed unless with written permission from the publisher. All rights reserved.

Table Of Contents

Introduction 4

Chapter 1: Embracing the geek's OS.....................................5

Chapter 2: The Top Linux Distributions 11

Chapter 3: The Rest of the Distro Gang............................. 13

Chapter 4: How to Choose the Right Distribution 18

Chapter 5: Desktop Environments: Do Looks Matter? 20

Chapter 6: The Lesser Known Desktop Environments 22

Chapter 7: All you need to get Linux running................... 24

Chapter 8: The Terminal: A Linux User's Best Friend 26

Chapter 9: The Don'ts.. 30

Chapter 10: 30 Linux Power-User Tips 32

Conclusion 42

Check Out My Other Books 43

Introduction

I want to thank you and congratulate you for purchasing the book, "Beginners guide to fast, easy and efficient learning of LINUX Operating Systems".

This book contains proven steps and strategies on how to start harnessing the power of the Linux operating system in your da-to-day computing needs.

If you are like 91.5% of the world, you are most likely using a Windows-based computer. Due to being a widely-supported operating system, Windows has been deemed by many to be the most user-friendly operating system of the bunch.

Or, you may be using Apple's OSX system -- hailed by many due to its very friendly learning curve and stability, as well as its supposed immunity to viral infections.

In comparison, the number of users who prefer Linux over these more mainstream operating systems can be considered to be in the decided minority. But the technological landscape is ever-evolving, and the age of the open-source is just around the river bend. Read this book to know all the basics of the most powerful free and open-source software -- Linux.

Thanks again for purchasing this book, I hope you enjoy it!

Chapter 1: Embracing the geek's OS

Over the years of its development, Linux has gained a reputation as a "geek's OS", mainly due to its interface. What many people neglect is the fact that Linux has caught up -- and in many places, surpassed -- its rivals. To introduce you to this, here are a few of the key differences between Linux and other OSes.

Access to the source.

Probably the most significant advantage of Linux over other prevalent OSes is the access to the source code. Linux belongs to the GNU Public license, ensuring that every single of its users can access and change the source code up to the very kernel *the foundation of any operating system). On the other hand, Windows and Apple do not allow users to even take a peek at the source code -- unless you are one of the select few who are in charge of its programming, or have the lucky break to be allowed to do so.

Users can look at this in two ways -- there are those who say that allowing the public to view and alter the operating system's code allows malicious programmers to take advantage of weaknesses that they may see. On the other hand, most Linux users see this as an opportunity to provide faster improvements and fixes. In fact, Linux has one of the fastest development rates among all existing operating systems, due to the fact that many people can view and tinker with the open source code at the same time. It is also noticeable that Linux does not have virus problems that are so prevalent on most other operating systems -- any person can run Linux for years on end and safely work without an antivirus software.

Freedom of license.

Most Internet users will agree -- there is nothing better than free. And Linux is the only operating system that can be legally obtained without spending a single penny. A person who obtains a GPL-licensed version of Linux has the freedom to change, republish, and even sell it as long as the code is made publicly available. Due to GPL, one can also obtain a single copy of Linux and install it on as many machines as one likes. In comparison, a single license of Windows or OSX allows a person to legally install that software on a single computer.

Speed of support.

Linux has the distinction of having a large peer support group online, via numerous forums. There are also several dedicated websites, and those who feel the need can purchase support contracts from a few of the bigger companies such as Red Hat and Novell.

Those who are not used to this support system may whine at the dozens of suggestions they may receive from the community in a short span of time from the moment of posting the problem. All of the most common problems with Linux are well documented, however, and it's very easy to find solutions quickly.

Peer support is also available for Windows and OSX, and there are just as many help sites and forums available. However, more advanced users can only be answered by Microsoft and Apple themselves -- and more often than not, paid support contracts need to be purchased in order to get such answers.

Hardware support.

In the olden days of Linux, many people criticized it due to poor hardware support. This means that if you wanted to install Linux on a computer, you would have to handpick each hardware component, lest the installation would not work.

Nowadays, however, such a problem is almost nonexistent. You can simply grab any computer running any operating system (unless it uses proprietary hardware like Apple almost always does) and convert it to Linux with minimal hiccups. Most Linux distributions eliminate the need to search for individual drivers every now and then if you happen to lose the hardware's install disk. Most hardware interfaces are also initially programmed using Linux, so compatibility can be inherent.

Command line usage.

One of the perceived advantages of Windows and Apple is the graphical user interface (GUI), that allows one to access every single command without going to the command prompt -- that intimidating white-on-black text-based window, that is a

Due to the advances in Linux's desktop environment, however, a user can also go on without ever touching the command line (called Terminal in Linux parlance). However, the Linux terminal is one of the most powerful tools ever created for administration purposes -- more powerful than any of its counterparts. Once one learns how to harness it (as you will at a later part of this book), it becomes the shortcut for a lot of confusing desktop work. Where else can you download and update several pieces of software at the same time, without going to the individual download pages?

Application Installation.

Every single Windows/Mac user will have encountered the pain of hunting for programs on individual web sites, purchasing the installers, and going through with the installation. For many years, this was thought to be easier than Linux's equivalent process -- which used to be right. However, that is not the case anymore.

With the terminal and the advent of such software as Synaptic package manager, you can simply open up a single tool and search for one or one dozen applications, and install them in just a click. This eliminates tedious web searching. This can also be used to remove other software versions that you no longer want.

On top of this, there is also a centralized repository for all Linux applications, via the Software Center. This is the GUI equivalent of the terminal command, which allows for fast and easy installation of new programs.

Flexibility.

While we have used the word "operating system" to describe Linux in general, it is in reality a misnomer (though we will continue using it for convenience). In fact, the term "Linux" can refer to any group of operating systems that can be applied almost anywhere. For computers, there are several "flavors" or distributions of the software: from the full-GUI capability of Ubuntu to the SD card-sized Puppy Linux. Linux is also the main kernel that runs the famous Android operating system for mobile devices, and it can be found in the firmware of such appliances as DVRs and televisions.

This flexibility extends not only to the software compatibility but also to its features. The Linux desktop is one of the most flexible desktop environments ever created -- you can make it look as flat as you want, with as little on it; you can also easily make it look like a sci-fi control screen, veering away from all semblance of a desktop environment.

Fanbase.

If you tell someone that you are a Linux user, many people will assume that you are a fanboy, someone recruiting people into your flock. This comes with good reason: Linux is one of those pieces of software that rely on word-of-mouth to gain users. Still tied to its school-project roots, Linux does not have the marketing budget of Windows or Apple.

This is in stark contrast to the corporate types backing rival OSes, who rely on the company mechanism to sell their software. As in other fields, corporate numbers and details are always less transparent than open-source fanboy ravings.

Removable Media handling.

Back in the days, every single removable media connected to the computer has to be mounted and unmounted in order for it to work or be removed. Nowadays, operating systems automatically mount the devices onto the computer, and a single click is all it takes to unmount. Many critics complain that Linux is lagging behind on this.

However, this is not entirely the case. Linux has been built (since its inception) as a multi-user platform. Most new Linux users (depending on the distribution used) gripe at the need to manually confirm the mounting of a device, but the removal of an "instant access" to inserted media is intentional in order to avoid overwriting the files of another user. This can be viewed as a failsafe -- when the inserted disk is automatically recognized, then what would stop another user from deleting or adding to the files already in your removable media?

Run levels.

This is a little bit technical, but still as important. Let's say that your Windows or Apple machine encountered a lethal hiccup, and you need to log into the OS's version of the Safe Mode in order to try and troubleshoot. Once you have done so, you are left with very little tools -- even the command prompt (if you get to it at all) does not provide much help. If you need, for example, to install a tool for diagnosis and fixing, the safe mode is not very friendly.

This is where Linux's ability to run at different run levels comes in handy. If you ever need to, you can run at "Level 3" -- that non-graphical mode that shows only the terminal. This mode has the same full access as the graphical "Level 5", allowing you to troubleshoot, or install a utility to do it for you.

The Open Source OS -- An Outline

Linux was the brainchild of Linus Torvalds, an operating system kernel that was fully introduced back in October 1991. Starting off in 1969 as Unix (and thus sharing the same ancestry as Apple's OSX), it was intended as a free operating system for Intel x86-based computers. Since its inception, it has gained the reputation as the most-ported operating system, being present in several computer hardware platforms.

Despite the prevalence of Windows and OSX in home computing, Linux has the lion's share when it comes to servers, supercomputers, and mainframes. This is mainly due to the flexibility, customizability, and generally low memory footprint of the OS that allows these devices to work at their best. Despite comprising only about 1.5% of desktop computers, it is typically seen on tablet computers, mobile phones, network routers, televisions, gaming consoles, and more. As previously mentioned, the most widely-used operating system for mobile devices (Android) is just a front for the Linux kernel. The software has also carved its exclusive niche in the film editing industry, in space applications, and even in some local and national government units.

Because of the General Public License, Linux comes packaged in hundreds of "distributions" with marked differences. These distros include the kernel, libraries and supporting utilities, and a built-in set of applications that meet the intended use of the distro. This final item has gained several Linux distributions popularity as grab-and-go operating systems.

Chapter 2: The Top Linux Distributions

As mentioned earlier, there are hundreds of Linux distributions. To the uninitiated, this can be a daunting selection. So we are listing only the top 5 (in no particular order) Linux distributions to help you get the one best suited to your needs.

Ubuntu. This is undoubtedly the most well-known distro ("flavor"), and is in itself based on another distro which is Debian. Though it has its own repositories (that place that stores software for your download), most of these are synched with Debian's.

Ubuntu focuses more on providing a solid server and desktop experience, building its own custom technology on the way. It uses its own "Unity" desktop environment, though previously it used a variant of the GNOME desktop environment (more on this later).

Ubuntu is also working on providing support for mobile devices. This flavor is for those who want to be on the leading edge of Linux (it offers new releases every half year), and those who look forward to a uniform experience whichever device they use.

Mint. This is basically a distro built right on top of Ubuntu. It uses the same repositories, so you have the same set of software available for either flavor. It gained popularity as a distro that included proprietary software and some media codecs that Ubuntu did not.

Mint is sometimes labeled as Ubuntu's lighter alternative, mostly due to its lighter desktop environment. This is also for those who are not keen on updates, as it does not automatically install them -- even the critical ones.

Debian. This Linux distribution is composed completely of free and open source software. The project has been operating since 1993, and they are still releasing newer versions (despite moving slower than either Ubuntu or Mint). This allows it to become both stable and conservative.

Fedora. This Linux project places a strong emphasis on free software in contrast with proprietary ones. In fact, there is no easy way of using proprietary graphic drivers on the system, even though third-party repositories are available. This distro is primarily for those who wish to be on the bleeding edge of development, who would like to have the latest versions as soon as they are out.

Fedora uses what they call "upstream" software, which is essentially stock software with minimal patches and custom tools. By default, it comes with the GNOME 3 desktop environment.

Red Hat Enterprise Linux (RHEL)/CentOS. This flavor is primarily for servers, workstations, and similar applications. It is based on Fedora, but is designed to be more stable with a long-term support.

However, the core software is open-source and free, Red Hat uses trademark to prevent it from being redistributed. In contrast, CentOS is a community project that strips Red Hat of its trademarks and makes the flavor available again for free use -- essentially RHEL's free counterpart. Recently, CentOS has become part of Red Hat itself.

Chapter 3: The Rest of the Distro Gang

Earlier, we mentioned that it was a difficult decision to filter out the top 5 distros. So in this chapter, we will present you with the rest of the most widely used Linux distros, again in no particular order.

openSUSE. This is a Linux distribution that has found a home not only among private users but also among commercial application. This flavor is based on the RPM package management system, which implements KDE as its main desktop environment. Despite this, it is flexible enough to offer GNOME, Mate, XFCE, LXDE, and a few others as installation options. The distro also offers a "rolling release" nicknamed the "Tumbleweed", as an alternative to its stable release. This is for those who want to have the latest version of openSUSE, including the unstable parts.

The flavor also includes YaST, a system management solution that comes with plenty of applications for those who wish to get started immediately. This is overall great for those users who wish to have a stable system, with a reliable support behind it.

Mageia. This distro was birthed from the Mandriva Linux back in 2010. Like some others, this uses the RPM system to manage the packages, and as such offers an assortment of desktop environments: Mate, RazorQt, Cinnamon, KDE, LXDE, GNOME, and XFCE can all be installed right from the DVD or from a repository. The newest Mageia system is planned to have the Btfrs file system as its default. Mageia is filled with a lot of helpful tools for customization and system setup, which is a fresh perspective if you want to walk away the many Ubuntu-based distributions and test something different.

This is best for those who want to swim outside the mainstream, and test a new distro that is both user-friendly and has a lot of desktop environments.

PC Linux OS. Also shortened to PCLOS, this has a reputation of being a simple Linux distribution supporting a lot of hardware right out of the box. This also includes some old devices, as well. The distro comes in two flavors, both of them lightweight: Mate and LXDE, which is the standard KDE desktop, plus a special edition nicknamed "FullMonty". The latter is a customized KDE edition, which has preinstalled applications as well as separate desktop environments depending on the activity -- Internet, Writing, Music, etc. This uses the RPM system to handle the repository, and has a lot of useful applications. This is a rolling release by default, so regular updates and new versions are to be expected.

This distro is best for the beginners who wish to have the latest software, as well as for those who do not want to sit for too long setting up the new installation.

Netrunner. This was created in 2010 and comes in two types: the Standard distribution which is based on Ubuntu, as well as the Rolling release based off Manjaro. It is focused on getting the user the best KDE experience, coming with a lot of useful applications as well as native apps for the KDE. It also offers beautiful themes, a simplified Systems dialog, and effects that are optimized for the lower-end machines. The flavor is also released as a Long Term Support, with periodical development releases.

This distribution is best for those users who want a simple, KDE-only system.

LXLE. This is a new player in the field of Linux distros, but it has already drawn attention thanks to its lightweight qualities. This is an Ubuntu-based model, having LXDE as its only desktop environment. It offers a very user-friendly transition for those who are on Windows or OSX, done through different "paradigms" that mimic the appearance of the other operating systems. Despite being lightweight and optimized for old systems, LXLE comes bundled with a lot of applications.

Overall, this flavor is for those who want to revive their old and ailing legacy machines, as well as for those who want to seamlessly move from either OSX or Windows.

Bodhi. This distro is specifically geared to be minimalist, and anti-bloat. In fact, it offers only a few applications upon setup, and will let the user choose what they wish to install via its own App Center. It also uses a unique lightweight DE, which is rarely seen in other flavors -- it is called "Enlightenment". This makes for a fast, stable, and customizable release. Its current edition is based off the Ubuntu Long Term Support.

This is mainly for those who wish to have just the basic set of applications, as well as those who want to put older computers to good use.

ElementaryOS. This is another Ubuntu distribution that puts simplicity and harmony above all else in its design and configuration. Out of the box, a basic set of applications can be installed plus an AppStore where others may be procured. It has its very own desktop environment dubbed the "Pantheon", which has a dock, an application launcher, and a panel.

This flavor is best suited for those who wish to have an OSX-lookalike that is very light on the machine's resources.

Manjaro. This takes Arch Linux's formidable power and bends it into a user-friendly approach. While KDE, Cinnamon, and GNOME are also available, the Manjaro flavor uses lightweight XFCE as its main desktop environment. The distro also offers auto-detection of hardware as well as the use of multiple kernels and hardware support. It also has its own repository, though the user can access and obtain software from the traditional Arch Linux repository. The user's system will always be up-to-date as it is a rolling release.

Manjaro is for those who want the latest system without having to go through too many steps to get their software. It is also for those interested in testing Arch Linux without having to go through the complexities of the full thing.

Korora. This is based in the Fedora system, though it provides multimedia codecs as well as third-party repositories. This makes the transition process simpler for new users. It has different "editions", such as KDE, GNOME, Cinnamon, XFCE, and Mate. Korora's primary goal is to make Fedora more appealing to more users, through including the popular apps by default. Its releases follow Fedora's.

The main strength of Korora lies in its multimedia support right out of the box, as well as its reputation for bringing Fedora to a more user-friendly plane.

Arch Linux. One of the more famous Linux distros, Arch Linux is also known for its power. However, one also needs to be very responsible in handling this power. Installing and setting up the distro requires advanced knowledge of the operating system, though several tutorials can help the beginner. Literally anything can be installed on this platform -- GNOME, Cinnamon, KDE, name it. There are also hundreds of applications one can get in the AUR (Arch User Repository). New snapshots are being released quite often for this rolling release distro, but one needs to be careful as sometimes these updates can break the system. In Arch Linux, you get to tweak and choose every single detail -- though there are official wiki and forums that can answer almost any question you might have.

This flavor is best enjoyed by those who prefer a minimalist setup, though it is also geared towards average to advanced users who want to learn more about Linux as a whole.

KaOS. This is a relatively young system that focuses on having all the fresh technologies and software. The newest release is a stable version sporting the latest KDE system. It sports its own software manager (dubbed the "Octopi"), and also has the lightweight browser QupZilla as its default. This flavor only works on 64-bit systems, though, so it can't be for everyone.

Despite the last point, KaOS is perfect for those average to advanced users who want to test out the latest in KDE technology.

Gentoo Linux. Gentoo has been praised by many pro Linux users for its unique philosophy -- instead of allowing the user to get pre-compiled programs for simple installation, it gets source codes instead. These source codes are then locally compiled so that the system can customize everything about the software and tailor them to the machine's specifics. This allows for a thoroughly native experience and can allow the programs to squeeze the very last ounce of power from the hardware.

On the other hand, Gentoo has not been characterized as beginner-friendly -- unlike much of the distros in this list, Gentoo does not have a graphical installer out of its Live Mode. Though there is a complete documentation on its handbook, it pretty much leaves the users with only the Internet and a command line at first.

Overall, this Linux flavor is geared towards highly experienced Linux users with old machines that they want to reuse.

Steam OS. Based on the Debian-Linux system, this is seen as the gamers' ultimate OS. Known as the title hub of choice for many gamers, Steam has ventured into the creation of their own Steam Machines, capable of running their take on Linux. However, this is not really a desktop variation -- it best works when connected to your living room television. Even though it is capable of working with programs and browsing the Web, it is best used by those living off the steam this online store provides. However, it is an interesting demonstration on how far the Free and Open Source philosophy of the Linux kernel can go.

Slackware. Our last entry for this chapter is a curiosity -- it is one of the first ever Linux distributions, and more than a decade after its initial release it is still going strong. For hardcore users, Slackware is just about as near as you can get to the proverbial "fast, stable, and secure". However, it has a major difference -- it offers virtually no GUI.

Slackware's hold on its many users rests on its infamous simplicity. Note that this does not mean "easy to use" but "stripped down and bare bones". This means that while Slackware has the steepest learning curve for people just getting into Linux, it is just the perfect thing for those Linux pros that can breeze through command lines.

Chapter 4: How to Choose the Right Distribution

Now that we have detailed the most common Linux distributions, it is time to actually decide which one you should use. The list in the previous two chapters is the farthest thing from exhaustive -- currently there are more than 600 different Linux distributions, and more are being made.

The defining factor of any Linux distribution is a lot more than just the look and feel of a desktop. While it may be true that you can simply choose to install and uninstall anything that does not suit your taste, you should always choose the distribution that is *closest to your preferred setup.* Here are a few things to consider:

Package managers. Different distros have different package managers. For example, while Debian and its derivatives use the Synaptic manager (which is very intuitive), some users prefer to use the command line where Fedora's yum manager excels.

Package availability. If you ever searched whether a particular software (or any of its kin) is available in Linux, then chances are good you will find it or its equivalent. But which Linux? There are some that are only available for Ubuntu, Arch, or Fedora. And then, some applications require a specific desktop environment (which again depends on the distro).

Stability vs Modernity. Many users tend to go for the most modern updates (such as rolling releases), but remember that this does not necessarily mean a better working environment. In fact, sometimes updating can introduce new bugs that compromise stability. This is why other systems such as Debian prefer to delay updates to make sure that things run a smoothly as possible. However, if you need something that stays at the cutting edge of Linux technology, then something with a rolling update (like Fedora) will work best.

Hardware compatibility. Different distributions offer different hardware support -- and these are often make-or-break points for users. While almost all distros can obtain any driver with added work on the user's part, this is not the ideal. It is always best to check out the performance of your distro with a Live CD so you know which hardware it will not support, if any.

Community support. And finally, there is the question of "What if I run into issues?" Linux is run in its entirety by the people who support it, and the larger the community is the more likely someone (or something, in cases of existing documentation) will be there to answer your questions.

As it is, you can always try out some of the "basic" distros so you know which suits you best (note that basic pertains to the fact that almost all other distros are derived from these). The standard will always be Ubuntu, which some consider to be the "poster boy" of the Linux movement. Then, for total beginners, there is Linux Mint. For those who are fond of the bleeding edge, there is Fedora. Those who value caution and stability will find Debian pleasing, while those who like to tinker will be happy with openSUSE. And finally, for those who want to take a deep dive into the whole Linux experience, there is ArchLinux.

Chapter 5: Desktop Environments: Do Looks Matter?

One of the most important aspects of different Linux distributions is the desktop environment -- earlier, we have demonstrated that this can be a major point of difference between distributions. This segment will explain more about how different desktop environments affect the overall performance of the distro.

GNOME (GNU Network Object Model Environment). Existing as the GNOME 3.x (but with living variations in lower numerical designations), GNOME is characterized by its simple and yet visually appealing image -- in fact, the latest GNOME environment looks and feels like the clean interface seen on today's mobile devices (though this may take some time to get used to on the desktop). There is a wealth of applications specifically designed for this desktop experience.

In order to run, GNOME requires a minimum of 768MB RAM and at least 400 MHz CPU. This makes it a bit more difficult for older systems.

UNITY. This was originally designed for use with netbooks, meaning it has less options for customization than even GNOME 2.x. This however has excellent synergy with touchscreen devices, which is useful for more modern laptop users. The appearance generally looks like the OSX desktop. Due to its features, it is quite heavy and requires at least a 1GB of RAM and 1GHz CPU in order to run smoothly.

CINNAMON. This desktop is more traditional than the other discussed, and is considered one of the most solid desktop environments. It looks closer to the GNOME 2.x series while still containing the technology behind the GNOME 3.x line. It is also lighter, requiring only 512 MB of RAM -- however, it needs a costly minimum of 1GHz CPU in order to run efficiently. A close cousin,

MATE, needs 200 MHz less in order to run but looks and feels essentially the same (minus the GNOME 3.x technology behind it).

KDE (K Desktop Environment). Those migrating from Windows to Linux will feel most at-home with this environment. Many would consider the KDE to be the most versatile and powerful desktop environment, with a feature called "Plasma Workspaces". This allows users to add widgets to the desktop for customization and utility. Without all the gizmos, it is also one of the most energy efficient -- thus, it is no surprise that this is the desktop environment of choice for distros geared for performance. Still, it would ned an optimum of 615 MB of RAM and 1 GHz of CPU to run at full blast.

XFCE. Even more performance-bent than KDE or Ubuntu, XFCE specializes on the conservation of system resources -- it only needs 192 MB of RAM and 300 MHz of CPU to run. This is considered by many to be the ideal blend between customization and system utilization. This very much resembles the clean look of Apple's OSX, so Mac immigrants will feel at home using it.

LXDE. This is the perfect solution for older computers, with only minimal system resource usage -- 128 MB of RAM, and 266 MHz of CPU. Distros wielding the LXDE desktop are by far the most portable of the lot, and are completely efficient when loaded on newer machines. It resembles the older Windows Operating Systems, but it does not completely sacrifice features -- it can still be customized more than any rival OS of its caliber. It is also good for beginners since it is very straightforward, with functional minimalism evident.

Chapter 6: The Lesser Known Desktop Environments

In the previous part, we have discussed some of the most famous desktop environments in Linux. But that is far from being a complete list -- in fact, there are dozens of other options the regular Linux user (even the near-expert ones) have never heard of. Here we will list hem -- it's just possible you might find an alternative that is more to your liking

xmonad. This is a tiling window manager, which means that it does not allow overlapping windows to be present on your desktop. This may take some time to sink in for those used to Windows, OSX, and the mainstream Linux flavors. This system basically does not allow you to drag and drop titlebars, since there are no titlebars to speak of. It does, however, allow for massive customization and allows systems to go much faster, which can increase your productivity.

Enlightenment. Older that the GNOME desktop environment, Enlightenment may be familiar to a few Linux users. It runs fast even on old systems, and also puts thought into its design principles. Those who are into futuristic-looking systems will enjoy using its interface.

ROX. This is a little on the weird side, as it supports the "everything is a file" philosophy that is the original idea behind UNIX-based systems while also taking ideas from the RISC OS. While many systems try to hide what goes on behind the hood and opt instead to have launchers and buttons facing the user, ROX takes the road less trodden and offers the entire file system for the user to tweak. In lieu with this, ROX uses the "applications are directories" method, putting all the support files and applications in a single directory -- which is finally treated as an app in itself..

Sugar. This desktop environment is geared for kids, placing heavy emphasis on their education. Apps will only run one at a time, always in fullscreen so there are no windows to manage.Also, there is neither a desktop nor a concept of "files". What Sugar has instead is a "Journal" that has the snapshots of applications and their saved states.

Étoilé. This is based on the GNUStep, which is the open source equivalent of the NeXT OpenStep system. This latter OS is the basis of Apple's proprietary Mac OSX. Due to this similarity, Mac powerusers may feel at home.This system takes the traditional high-level route, which hides many of the system complexities.

Ratpoison. Ratpoison was named as such for a reason -- it kills your mouse dead. This environment relies on the keyboard for anything and everything, and as such has a bit of a learning curve. Once the user gets over it, however, Ratpoison is easily one of the fastest, most stable, most customizable desktop environments. Security is also something that would not be much of a problem -- most people would likely not even know how to open a file if ever they get their hands on your computer.

UDE. Short for Unix Desktop Environment, this is based on Xlib and is hence easy to port to different systems. This desktop does not sport any title bars on its windows,and there are no close or minimize buttons. Instead, it has what is called the "Hex Menu" , that can be triggered by clicking on the border of the windows. UDE is also heavy on the mouse, and in some instances will require a three-button mouse in order to work at full power.

Mezzo. This desktop environment is different, simply because it is one of those that do not have menus and submenus that can be used to categorize and launch applications. Instead, there are different general system tasks attached to each of the four corners of the screen (such as Programs or Files). This has the goal of simplifying the interaction between the user and the system. This desktop environment has been primarily used in SymphonyOS.

AmiWM. This is a very simple window manager whose goal is to emulate the Amiga Workbench. There is even a patch that can make it look like the original Amiga Workbench versions.

Awesome. This is another tiling window manager that is both highly configurable and extensible. The extensions are done using the Lua scripts. Just like Ratpoison, one does not need a mouse when running this and multiple monitors are supported very well. The minimalist design also makes this desktop environment lightning fast.

Chapter 7: All you need to get Linux running

We are giving this tutorial assuming that you have a different operating system installed at this moment. One of the advantages of Linux is that you do not actually have to install it in order to experience the difference. Almost all of the major Linux distributions are available in a "Live CD" format -- all you have to do is mount the removable device that has the installer and boot from it (this usually requires you to press a key such as F2, F12, or DEL depending on the machine manufacturer). Afterwards, you will be able to see an option that allows you to launch it instead of installing -- you can now take your Linux distro for a spin! If you don't like it, simply reboot your computer and remove the media.

Once you have decided to completely go through with the Linux installation, it is time to start migrating your current files to make sure they will not be deleted during installation. Any backup solution that copies your files is okay -- in fact, it is highly recommended that you back up your files to multiple sources (the Cloud, a DVD, an external hard drive, etc.) so you have multiple restore sources in case one fails.

Fortunately, installing Linux is almost always a one-click deal. Simply restart the computer and boot from the removable media again, but this time select the "Install" option. The process will start and may need simple inputs from you from time to time (such as the location, language, keyboard preference, etc.). You can also initiate this by choosing the "Install" option on the desktop of the Live CD mode. If an existing operating system is detected, you will usually (depending on the distro) be given the option to install Linux in a "dual boot" configuration, meaning it will run alongside whatever OS you have right now.

Towards the end of the installation, a very important screen will pop up: the password prompt. Make sure to choose a password that is both complicated and easy to remember (or at least make sure you have a secure backup of it). This password will serve as your "sudo" or "root" password, the most important password in the system that allows you to do advanced tasks. On the same screen, you will also be asked for a computer name (what the system calls your device) and a username (what your system calls you).

Once you have completed these steps, reboot your computer and restore the files to your drive -- your new Linux installation is ready to use! Right out of the box, you should be able to see lots of different software that can handle just about any basic computing needs.

Browsing, Installing, Uninstalling, and Updating Software

One of the most intriguing aspects of Linux is its uniquely advanced approach to software management. Aside from the terminal, each Linux distro is also equipped with a Software Center that contains all the programs that can be installed on your machine. This means that you can simply search for the name (or a part of it), and the program will show up instantly. You can either install it from there (if you do not yet have it), update it, or remove it.

Chapter 8: The Terminal: A Linux User's Best Friend

Among all other operating systems, Linux users stand out due to one thing -- they learn to love the terminal. This is despite the initial revulsion thrown at the white-on-black interface -- after all, most of us grew up with Windows' and OSX's graphical user interface.

But as mentioned before, the Linux terminal is extremely powerful. While the most effective way to learn to use it is to use it firsthand, we will be showing you some of the basic and most useful terminal commands.

The terminal may be launched by a desktop shortcut, or through a keyboard shortcut (which varies depending on the distribution). Once you launch it, you are likely to see the "bash" shell, the command shell that most Linux flavors use. You will see that it already contains a line in the following syntax:

username@computername:~$

Launching a program

This is especially useful if you have more than a dozen applications. Simply type the application name, like so:

Firefox

The above command launched the Firefox web browser (which comes built-into almost all Linux distros. Notice that you did not need to add any file extensions, as programs do not have file extensions in Linux.

If you are opening a web browser, there is a plus -- you can immediately direct it to open a specific website after starting. Simply type the web address right after the program name:

Firefox amazon.com

This commands the system to launch Firefox and go to Amazon's website.

Installing a software

You can also use the terminal to install any number of software at once (provided they are available in the universal repository). While the exact command may again vary depending on the distribution, the most common command is as follows:

Sudo apt-get install packagename

where packagename is the name of the program you wish to install. The system will prompt you for your "sudo" password. This may appear complicated at first, but this is in fact very convenient. For example, you would like to install three packages at once:

Sudo apt-get install package1 package2 package3 package4

If you do not know the exact name of the package you want to install, you can use the tab completion trick that will be discussed later.

Files and Directories

By default, the terminal looks in the home directory unless you specify another one. In order to specify a different directory and access a specific file, simply follow the following syntax:

Drive1/folder1/folder2/folder3/documentname

If you specify a path/document that does not exist, the system, will usually create a new file at the location you specified.

Here are a few other basic commands you will find handy:

Cd - the "~" to the left of the prompt represents the home directory, the default directory for almost all distros. Use the "cd" command to change to a different directory. For example:

Cd/home/folder1

would change the directory to "folder1". Adding ".." after the "cd" command would have the terminal go up a directory.

Ls - The "ls" command is handy for listing all the files in the specified directory.

Mkdir - This commands makes a new directory. For example:

Mkdir folder1

Would create a new directory called "folder1" in the current directory.

Rm - This removes a specified file. For example:

Rm file1

removes the file named "file1" in the current directory.

Cp - The command copies a file in the current directory to a different directory. For example:

cp file1 /drive1/folder1/folder2

copies the file named "file1" to the "folder1" directory.

Mv - This command is used to move a file from one directory to another, working exactly like the "cp" command above. However, it can also be used to rename files:

Mv originalfile newfile

effectively moves "originalfile" into "newfile", thereby renaming it.

Tab Completion

This is a very useful trick when you do not know exactly what filename or package name you are looking for. For example, you are trying to install the Firefox browser -- you can simply type the first few letters and hit the Tab key in order to complete it! This works for all programs in the software repository as well as all programs in the current directory.

There are a lot of cases when the system cannot tell what you are trying to type because there are multiple matches. Simply hit the Tab key again to see a list of the possible matches. You can continue typing to narrow down the list, then hit Tab again to complete the entry.

Chapter 9: The Don'ts

The terminal may become so much a part of your Linux experience that you may seek to solve difficult problems by using terminal commands. In the process, you may come across helpful folks giving out advice -- but remember, never run a terminal command unless you know exactly what it will do! Remember that as long as you are running on root (i.e., you have entered the sudo password), you will no longer receive warning prompts whatever you try to do -- even if it kills the system. To help you out, here are seven sins -- terminal commands that you should never run no matter what.

Rm -rf / - This command deletes everything -- from your hard drive to connected media devices! In effect, it tells the system to recursively delete everything starting from the root directory.

Variations of the same command include - rm -rf~ and rm -rf .*.

:(){ :|: & };: - This short and weird function is basically a "denial of service" attack, called by many as the "Fork Bomb". This basically outlines a shell function that continually replicates itself, taking up all your computer resources in a very short span of time.

Mkfs.ext4 /dev/sda1 - This command formats your hard drive -- essentially, this tells Linux to create an entirely new ext4 (the file system Linux uses) on the first hard drive, which is more often than not the drive in use.

Command > /dev/sda - This is a syntax where "command" can be any command. This sends the output of that command directly to the hard drive, writing over it and damaging it.

Dd if=/dev/random of=/dev/sda - This command writes junk onto the hard drive that may be lethal to your system. It copies random data to the first hard disk, thereby corrupting it.

Mv ~ /dev/null - The "null" part of this command is essentially a blackhole -- moving anything to it consigns it to oblivion. This command in effect moves your entire home folder to that blackhole, destroying your files.to that blackhole, destroying your files.

Chapter 10: 30 Linux Power-User Tips

In this chapter, you will be shown the power of Linux through 30 tips that will essentially turn you into a power user. Read on and see how these can make your life so much easier!

1. Checking all processes that are not run by you.

If you are using a terminal connected to a mainframe, you are essentially sharing resources with other users on the same system as you. This means that when they go over the top with their processes, your speed might get affected as well.

In order to identify processes you didn't start, simply type the following command on the terminal:

ps aux | grep -v `whoami`

You may also want to just list the top 10 activities hogging the resources:

ps aux --sort=-%cpu | grep -m 11 -v `whoami`

It would be advisable to run these commands as root so that you can filter out the vital background processes that could not be terminated anyway. If you notice something that shouldn't be there, you can now kill the process and regain your rightful right to system resources!

2. Replacing text in multiple documents

There may be times when you want to change all instances of a specific text throughout different locations. This can easily be done through the terminal. Let's say you will be changing all instances of the word "book" with "ebook" in the current directory (called "sample"), just type and run the following:

Perl -i -pe 's/bool/ebook/;' sample

If you want this change to be done just across all text files within the sample directory, this line would be helpful:

Find . -name '.txt' -print | xargs perl -pi - e's/book/ebook/ig' *.txt*

You can also try the following, which will work on regular files:

Find -type f -name ".txt' -printo | xards --null perl -pi -e 's/book/ebook/'*

3. Fixing a malfunctioning Terminal

Regardless of how stable the bash terminal is, there are time when we perform accidental commands that can mess things up. An example is when cat is used to list a file, and a binary equivalent ends up on screen. There might also be beeping funny characters, or abnormal color combinations. In these cases, all one has to do is to send an initialization command:

Reset

After this, everything should be back to normal.

4. Creating keywords on Mozilla Firefox

For those who have used the Konqueror browser, many have found great convenience in the fact that you can simply type the words "gg Linux" on the box to initiate a Googel search on the word Linux. But Firefox is the default Internet browser appearing on most of the Linux distros, and it is in a power-user's interest to finetune Mozilla's product to their advantage -- even emulating this function from Konqueror.

First, click on the Bookmarks option then follow up with Manage Bookmarks. Click on Add a New Bookmark, then add the URL as the following:

http://www.google.com/search?q=%s

After this, select the entry within the bookmark editor menu, and click on the Property button. Enter the search keyword as "gg" (you may substitute this for any other combination of your preference). This completes the process -- the %s in the URL you have placed earlier will automatically be replaced by the text right after the keyword. This can also be used for any other site that relies on the browser passing the search/activity information onto the URL.

You can also use a second way, which is to right-click on the search field and to select the "Add a Keyword for this Search" option. Then, the following dialog box will allow you to use your specific keyword.

5. Running Multiple Applications of a Program

There are times when you miht be sharing your workstation with someone, and you are both working on different projects on the same program Assuming that the Linux system is running on graphical mode (run level 5), the user can press the Ctl+Alt+F1 prompt to get a prompt for log in. Simply run the following:

Startx -- :1

where x is the program. This gets you into the graphical environment. In order to go back to the previous session, just press Ctrl+Alt+F7. Finally, to get back to the session that you were using, you can simply hit the following key combination: Ctrl+Alt+F8. This trick can be repeated by the keys F1 to F6, which can identify six different console sessions.

As a caveat, though, this trick might not be running in each and every distro out there so best check first.

6. Get faster browsing

In a KDE environment, there is a simple useful option that can speed up the entire browsing experience. Simply start whatever Control System you have by going to System and then KDE on the sidebar. Once this is done, select to have Konqueror preloaded in instances. This means that the software will run on startup, but will be kept hidden until one attempts to use it.

7. Easily backup a full website

This is handy especially if you want to save an entire directory on a computer, and then have only the changed files sent to each background, instead of having everything copied. The rsync tool can call this, but you will need to have an account using the latest system you will be tapping into:

Rsync -vare ssh user@192.168.0.2:/home/test/important/ /home/test2/backup*

The above section shows how we are able to back up all the files from

192.168.0.2's "important" folder to the current test2 directory.

8. Keeping the clock on time

There are times when the built-in clock on your computer wanders off the mark due to minute inconsistencies. This can easily be rectified using the terminal. In fact, you can make use of a special NTP tool that makes sure you are always nearly perfectly synchronized with the time. Simply use the following command on your terminal:

Ntpdate ntp.blueyonder.co.uk

You can also look up a list of suitable servers for NTP synch. If boot processes and scripts are then modified to include this command, one can ensure that the machine is always on time from the moment of booting. A cron job may also be ran to update the system time.

9. Searching for the biggest files

Sometimes we put too much in our hard drives and we forget which files are hogging the most space. These files can be audio/video clips, or just about anything else. Instead of fussing over individual lists, you can simply type this in the terminal:

Ls -lSrh

The "r" portion will cause the large files to be listed at the very end. The "h" part, on the other hand, gives a human readable output including the size and other details.

You can also narrow down your search. Say you want to include only the biggest MPEGs in the list, you can use:

*Ls -lSrh *.mp**

If you want to look at a higher level and find the largest directories, you can also do so:

Du -kx | egrep -v "\./.+/" | sort -n

10. Making shortcuts for Nautilus

Most file managers, regardless of the distro, are used with the mouse. There are those from another era, however, that rely almost solely on keyboards. While they may seem cumbersome at first, these offer nearly unparalleled file-browsing efficiency. One such manager is Nautilus. Using this program, you can do the following with just a hotkey:

Open a parent folder = Ctrl+Up arrow

Open a specific location = Ctrl+L

Navigate around the folder = Arrow keys

The file icons can also be customized using "emblems". These are basically graphical overlays that can be applied to the files, either as a group or individually. Simply open the Nautilus' Edit menu and click on Backgrounds and Emblems. In this interface, you will be able to drag-and-drop the images.

11. Defragment the database

This is especially useful if you are using MySQL for any reason on your Linux machine. When a structure of this type of database is changed, or if a lot of data has been removed, a loss of performance may arise from the resulting fragmentation. This is especially noticeable when running queries. At this point, you may use the following command to run the optimizer:

Mysqlcheck -o <database>

where "<database>" refers to the name of the database you wish to defragment. If you are using VARCHAR fields, then it would be advisable to run this command every once in a while. Variable-length columns like these are actually prone to fragmentation.

12. Make emails faster

If you are on KDE and you can't live without sending a mountain of email messages in an hour, you're in luck -- sending an email using this desktop environment is just a few key presses away. Simply bring up the "run command" by pressing Alt+F2. Then, type:

Mailto: <email address>

where <email address> is where you'd like to send the message to. After hitting the Enter key, the command will launch KMail, which will then be ready to receive the message. There is no need to fill the

entire email address. This shortcut will also work with website URLs -
- typing a URL in the box will launch the default KDE browser (in
many cases, Konqueror).

13. Save battery

The "hdparm" command is great for tuning hard drives, but it also
can be used to save battery life on a laptop. It can also make you a
little more productive by toning down the fierce hard drive whirring.

Type the following into the terminal:

Hdparm -y /dev/hdb

Hdparm -y /dev/hdb

Hdparm -S 36 /dev/hdb

These commands tell the system to do the following in order: set the
hard drive to Standby, transition into Sleep mode, and lastly enter the
timeout for the Automatic spindown. The last line includes a certain
numeric variable, where each unit equals 2 seconds (a minute is 12
units).

14. Manage wireless speeds

Of course, one of the primary determinants for the success of radio
transmission/reception is the amount of signal that is available. So
that the communication can remain even when the signal starts to
fade, a slower rate of data transmission needs to be implemented.
Usually, radios will attempt to work out the available signal and select
the fastest possible speed on their own.

But in areas that have barely adequate signal, valuable packets of data
may be lost while there is a continuous renegotiation of the link
speed. If the equipment cannot be repositioned or if no antenna gain
can be added, forcing the card to sync at a lower rate can cause better
signal reception. This will mean fewer retries, and can be faster than
an in-and-out communication. This can be done through the
following command:

Iwconfg eth0 rate2M

This will force the radio to always set the sync speed at 2Mbps, despite the availability of other speeds. A particular speed may also be a ceiling, allowing the card to scale to slower speeds but limiting the fastest it can go. An example is:

Iwconfig eth0 rate 5.5M auto

This directive will force the card to allow sync speeds of up to 5.5Mbps, but not faster than this. For those who want to restore the basic auto-scaling ability of the cards, simply specify the "auto" function again:

Iwconfig eth0 rate auto

Remember that cards can usually reach further at lower speed than at a higher speed. For example, some cards have gain difference of 12dB (four times the potential) when they drop the speeds from 11Mbps to 1 Mbps.

15. Faster Hard Drives

If you have not yet used hdparm to optimize your hard disk, now is the time. The command is very powerful, and can turn on some features that by default are disabled. Before starting, however, remember that these changes can very easily lead to data corruption -- meaning, any important data should be backed up.

First, do a speed test using the following command:

Hdparm -Tt /dev/hda

Something such as the following can be seen:

/dev/hda:

Timing buffer-cache reads: xxxxxxx

Timing buffer disk reads: xxxxxxx

These values will show the current hard drive speeds. From here, you can try speeding things up. Find out what options are currently being used by the drive, through passing the hdparm on the device's name:

Hdparm /dev/hda

You will find a fairly default setting, as a lot of distros will opt for safer options known to work with most hardware. In order to get more speed, you would want to enable the dma mode, as well as make certain adjustments on the input/output support. A lot of modern computers would support "mode 3", a 32-bit mode of transfer that can almost double the throughput. To do this, try:

Hdparm -c3 -dl/dev/hda

After this, try rerunning the speedcheck to see if the settings applied. Remember to counter-check the modes the hardware will support, as well as the hdparm man pages in order to know how to set them.

16. Accessing programs remotely

If you ever wished you can lie with your Linux device and remotely access the applications on your Windows machine, then you can do so now. This is through SSH. Just enable the following in the /etc/ssh/sshd_config

XllForwarding yes

Now, you can use GIMP to remote-view your applications:

Ssh -X <IP address> gimp

where <IP address> is that of the machine you wish to remote-view.

17. Unlock Emacs secret modes

The Emacs is never just a text editor -- in fact, it can be the perfect thing to light up those boring moments. Want to talk to someone? Open up Emacs, hit the Esc key, and then the letter x. Type in the word "doctor" -- and Emacs will transform into an underskilled therapist ready to listen to your troubles. Or, maybe you want to call up an old arcade favorite -- type in "tetris" right after the Esc-X combination, and Emacs will oblige!

You can actually check out the package list of the distro to see what they have bundled for your version of Emacs. Some versions can have chess, IRC chat, Perl integration, HTML conversion, French translation, smart compilation, a Java IDE, and a curious thing called "semantic bovinator".

18. Unmounting busy drives

You will be familiar with that situation when you are trying to unmount a certain drive, but you are always being told by your system that that drive is busy. So what application is tying up the device? This should tell you:

Lsof +D /mnt/windows

This should return the command (as well as the process ID) that is connected to the task accessing your /mnt/windows directory. They can then be located, or the kill command can be used to finish them off.

19. Listing files that have been done today

If you are using your Linux system to work with a variety of files, this may come in handy. There will always be that time when you created a file earlier in the day, and the file is suddenly required later on. The thing is, you do not know exactly what you put in that filename... and your home folder is an unorganized mess of several hundred files. There are various ways out of this predicament, but this in one of the most efficient, utilizing the power of shell commands:

Ls -al --time-style=+%D | grep 'date +%D'

The command shows the parameters to the ls command, which causes the output to be set in a particular format. The good part is that the output is then passed on to the grep command, which will substitute the date into the string that would be matched. This can easily be modified to search for other dates, filesizes, times, or whatever.

20. Avoid long commands and typing mistakes

This technique can be used to create a shortcut for almost any other command in this chapter -- and it can also be used for more clever ideas. Let's try the previous technique we used and shorten it with a new "lsnew" command:

Alias lsnew=" ls -al --time-style=+%D | grep 'date +%D' "

This can also be used to do a sort of terminal-limited autocorrect. For example, when typing to change to the parent directory, you might be in a habit of leaving out the space. Hence, you can create a new shortcut:

Alias cd.. =" cd .."

You can also rewrite a few existing commands, such as:

Alias ls="ls -al"

This will save a few keypresses here and there. Finally, in order to have all of these command shortcuts enabled for each session, just add the commands to the .bashrc file within the home directory.

21. Change Mozilla's secret settings.

There are times when we want to change the way Firefox works, but find no way to access in-depth options in the clickable GUI. In fact, there is a special mode that will help you gain better control. Simply type this option into the address bar:

About:config

This will show the different settings that can be changed, and you can alter them using the value fields in the table.

There are also other interesting modes, that include the general information (about:), different details about plugins (about:plugins), information about credits (about:credits), and some general words of wisdom (about:mozilla)

22. Opening an SVG file directly

A user can run Inkscape directly from the shell and edit any graphic directly from its URL. Simply type:

Inkscape <SVG URL>

Remember, though, to save it as something else.

23. Editing without editors

There are some very long files that may be hard to manipulate using a traditional text editor. If this task needs to be done every day, then it could be much easier to use command-line tool instead. Here are some examples.

To print columns 3 and 7 from a file (say, file 1) into a different one (file 2), the following can be used:

Awk '{print $3, $7}' file1>file2

To output just characters from column9 into column 10 of the same file (file1), the cut command can be used:

Cut -c 9-10 file1>file2

To replace all instances of a word (word1) with (word2), the sed command can be used:

Sed "s/word1/word2/g" file1>file2

These will usually be faster than opening and working with a text editor.

23. Backing up only selected files

Tar can be used to bahckup only certain files in a directory. The -t flag can be used, ut you must first create a file with the file that needs to be backed up. Type in the following commands:

Cat >> /etc/backup.conf

 # /etc/file1

3 /etc/file1

 # etc/file3

 # etc/sfile4

EOF

Then, run the tar command and have the -T flag point to the file that was just created:

Tar -cjf bck-etc-'date+%Y-%m-%d'.tar.bz2- T /etc/backup.conf

After this the backup should already be created.

24. Case sensitivity

Despite word cases not making any difference at all in other operating systems, the words "Command" and "command" in Linux are entirely different animals. This difference can cause trouble since files moved between Windows and Linux may respond differently. There is, thankfully, a shell utility that can be used to change the cases of different files.

#!bin/bin/sh

For i in 'ls -l'; do

  Filex='echo $i | tr [A-Z] [a-z]

  Mv 4i $filex 2>/dev/null

Done

where "filex" is the name of the file in question. After this is executed, the names "FILE1" and "FiLE2" will be changed to lowercase versions.

25. Killing spam

Spam is still a widespread problem, evidenced by its presence in any system. The good news is that setting up an anti-spam system locally can greatly augment the spam filter already in place with your ISP and email provider. This is done through KMail.

You can create a quick and easy filter to bin for your mail, or direct the name to a junk folder. This can be done since the header includes the spam label, though the exact one used can depend on the ISP.

Create a filter in the program, choose the "Match Any of the Following" option and then type the header details as well as the action that you wish to be performed. Set this filter so it applies to all incoming mail, and you should have a stronger and more versatile anti-spam system.

26. Finding where a certain drive mounted

Sometimes you might have a lot of mountable devices, including flash memories, key drives, etc.). Because of this, it could be different to know where that device you just plugged in ended up.

All devices inserter into a drive invoke a driver -- such as "usb-storage" -- and will dump some useful information within the logs. You can try typing:

Dmesg | grep SCSI

This is supposed to filter out the recognized drive specs from the output of dmesg. A certain text may return that states where the device is mounted (e.g., sda)

27. Securely log out

When the console is being used on a shared device, or even on your own desktop that someone borrows for the time being, you will find that the screen will show a trace of who was last to log in and what they were doing even after logging out. While some distros no longer have this, some still do. This can be solved by editing the ~/.bash_logout file, adding the "clear" command. Other commands may also be added here.

28. Backing up a package list on Debian

If you are on Debian, there is an easy way to backup all currently installed packages even when you have lost track of them. First, you can get the list by running the following commands:

Dpkg - -get-selections>debianlist.txt

This will list out all packages in a file called "debianlist.txt". Then, the same packages can be installed on a different computer with the following:

Dpkg - -set-selections < debianlist.txt

Remember that aside from these, you also have to copy configuration files from /etc when the system is being copied to a new computer.

To install the selections, use the following command:

Apt-get -u dselect-upgrade

29. Hardening the SSH

The SSH is actually a secure way to connect to a server, but there are two changes that can be made to improve this. First, any normal user would not want any person being able to log in as root -- they should only be able to log on as a normal user, after which they can use the su command to switch. This can be changed in the /etc/ssh/ssh_config file -- simply add the following line to it:

PermitRootLogin no

This way, the only access root priveleges would be through su -- which further means that hackers have to break two different passwords to get root access.

While the file is being edited, find also the line which says "Protocol 2, 1" and then change it to simply "Protocol 2". This will remove the option to have the system fallback on the original protocol for SSH. This original protocol is nowadays considered very vulnerable.

30. KDE housekeeping upon log out

If you are a Windows migrant, you will remember that there are a lot of different programs on that OS that can clean the web cache, take out temporary files, and other things when you log out. The cool thing is that all these can be done on the KDE environment without even installing programs -- the startkde script will automatically execute scripts that have been placed in special places.

First of all, you will need to create a "shutdown" directory in the .kde directory. This is done through the following:

Mkdir /home/username/.kde/shutdown

You can now create the script that will perform customized actions upon shutdown. These actions can include cleaning up the temp folders, the caches, and the form autocompletes. Save it under any name (such as "cleanup.sh"). Afterwards, make sure that the correct permissions are set up:

Chmod ug+x ~/.kde/shutdown/cleanup.sh

If you do not know which one's your default KDE directory, you can try the following command:

Kde-config - -path exe

Conclusion

Thank you again for purchasing this book!

I hope this book was able to help you to get a leg up on using Linux.

Linux is undoubtedly the most powerful and yet most misunderstood of all the major operating systems. While many people shy away from it, it is in everyone's self-interest to learn it and use it for their day-to-day needs. This ebook aimed to show anyone even the least bit curious how Linux would fit into their daily routine -- and remarkably so!

The next step will be to actually experience Linux for yourself. You have everything you needed right in this book -- Linux is an adventure, and by now you should be up for it!

Finally, if you enjoyed this book, please take the time to share your thoughts and post a review on Amazon. We do our best to reach out to readers and provide the best value we can. Your positive review will help us achieve that. It'd be greatly appreciated!

Thank you and good luck!

Check Out My Other Books

Below you'll find some of my other popular books that are popular on Amazon and Kindle as well. Simply click on the links below to check them out. Alternatively, you can visit my author page on Amazon to see other work done by me.

C Programming Success in a Day

Android Programming in a Day

Python Programming in a Day

PHP Programming Professional Made Easy

CSS Programming Professional Made Easy

Windows 8 Tips for Beginners

If the links do not work, for whatever reason, you can simply search for these titles on the Amazon website to find them.

www.ingramcontent.com/pod-product-compliance
Lightning Source LLC
Chambersburg PA
CBHW071010180526
45168CB00003B/1369